Collages from the

Book of

Revelation

by Margaret Raftery

ISBN: 978-0-578-82275-4

In Memory of

Immaculate Heart College
and my Art Teachers

Margaret Martin (1910–1995)

and

Corita Kent (1918–1986)

Artist Statement

The Book of Revelation is a very relevant book for our modern
world. I have illustrated the Book of Revelation with collages made
from National Geographic magazines and also old Life magazines.
My collages are giving a visual image to the Word of God.
Biblical quotes are taken from the Revised Standard Version
of Bible by Ignatius Press Revised 1957 Catholic Edition.

I John your brother ... was on the island called Patmos on account of the word of God and testimony of Jesus. I was in the Spirit ... and I heard behind me a loud voice like a trumpet 'saying' write what you see in a book and send it to the seven churches. Now write what you see, what is and what is to take place.

Rev. 1:9–11

And all the churches shall know that I am he who searches mind and heart, and I will give to each of you as your work deserve.

Rev. 2:23

Remember then what you received and heard, keep that and repent ... I will come like a thief and you will not know at what hour I will come ... He who has an ear, let him hear what the Spirit says to the churches.

Rev. 3:3, 6

After this I looked, and lo,
in heaven an open door! And the
first voice, which I heard
speaking to me like a trumpet,
said 'Come up hither, and
I will show you what must
take place after this.' At once
I was in the Spirit, and lo,
a throne stood in heaven, with
one seated on the throne!

Rev. 4:1–2

10-18-19 MR

Who is worthy to open
the scroll and break its seals?
Weep not: lo the Lion of the tribe
of Judah, the Root of David has
conquered so that he can open
the scroll and its seven seals.

Rev. 5:2, 5

Now I saw when the Lamb opened one of the seven seals ... a white horse ... and he went out conquering and to conquer. When he opened the second seal ... out came another horse, bright red; its rider was permitted to take peace from the earth. When he opened the third seal I saw a black horse and its rider had a balance in his hand; saying 'a quart of wheat for a denarius.' When he opened the fourth seal ... I saw a pale horse and its rider's name was Death.

Rev. 6:1–8

When he opened the sixth seal
I looked, and behold, there was
a great earthquake: and the sun
became black as sackcloth,
the full moon became like blood,
and the stars of the sky fell
to earth ... the sky vanished
like a scroll that is rolled up.

Rev. 6:12–14

After this I looked, and behold
a great multitude which no man
could number, from every nation,
from all tribes and peoples
and tongues, standing before
the throne and before the Lamb.

Rev. 7:9

*When the Lamb opened
the seventh seal, there was silence
in heaven ... I saw seven angels
who stand before God and seven
trumpets were given to them.*

Rev. 8:1–2

And the fifth angel blew
his trumpet, and I saw a star
fallen from heaven to earth.
And in those days men will
seek death and will not find it.

Rev. 9:1, 6

There should be no more
delay, but that the days
of the trumpet call to be
sounded by the seventh angel,
the mystery of God, as he
announced to his servants the
prophets should be fulfilled.

Rev. 10:6–7

*Then God's temple in heaven
was opened, and the ark
of his covenant was seen
within his temple, and there
were flashes of lightning,
voices, peals of thunder,
an earthquake and heavy hail.*

Rev. 11:19

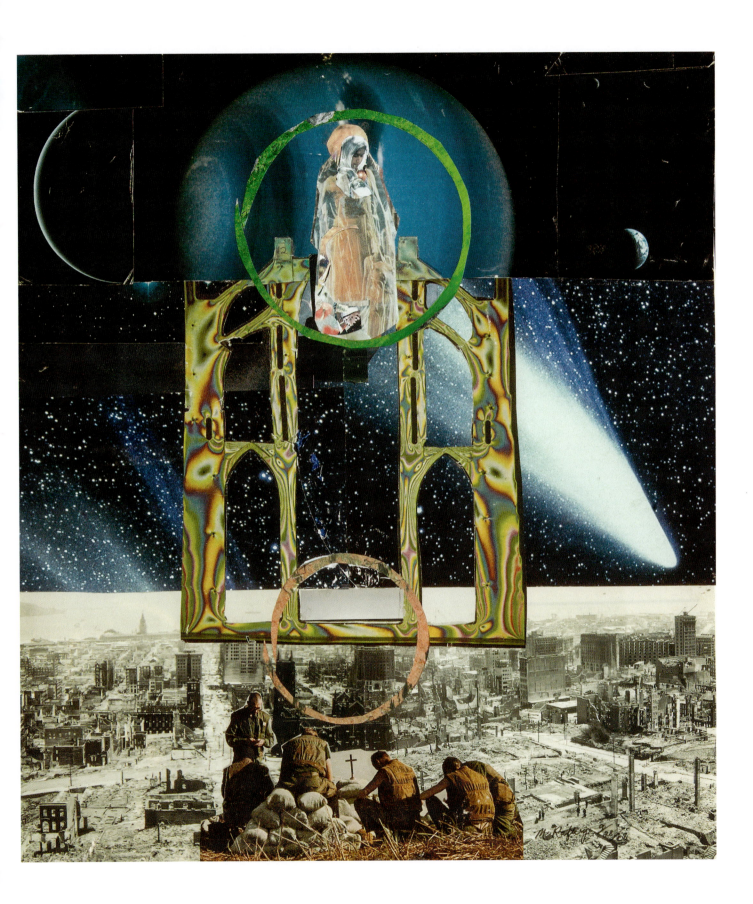

And a great portent
appeared in heaven, a woman
clothed with the sun, with
the moon under her feet,
and on her head a crown of
twelve stars; she was with child.

Rev. 12:1–2

HAIL, HOLY QUEEN
Hail, Holy Queen, Mother of ... our life, our sweetness ... our hope.

Now war arose in heaven, Michael and his angels fighting against the dragon; and the dragon and his angels fought, but they were defeated ... And when the dragon saw that he had been thrown down to the earth, he pursued the woman who had borne the male child. But the woman was given the two wings of the great eagle that she might fly from the serpent into the wilderness ... Then the dragon was angry with the woman, and went off to make war on the rest of her offspring.

Rev. 12:7–9, 13–17

And I saw a beast rising out of the sea ... and to it the dragon gave his power and his throne and great authority ... Men worshipped the dragon, for he had given his authority to the beast ... Then I saw another beast which rose out of the earth ... it works great signs even making fire come down from heaven to earth in the sight of men ... it deceives those who dwell on the earth.

Rev. 13:1–4, 11, 13–14

Then I looked, and lo, on Mount Zion stood the Lamb and with him a hundred and forty-four thousand who had his name and his Father's name written on their foreheads ... And they sing a new song before the throne and before the four living creatures and before the elders.

Rev. 14:1, 3

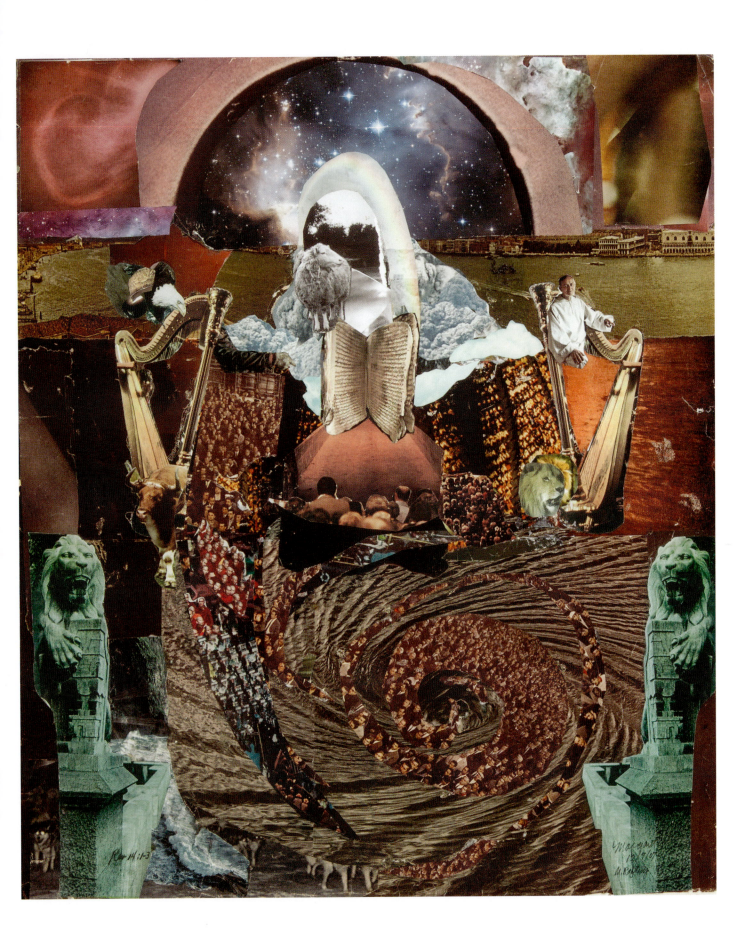

Fear God and give him glory, for the hour of his judgement has come. If any one worships the beast and its image, and receives a mark on his forehead or on his hand, he also shall drink the wine of God's wrath. And I heard a voice from heaven saying write this ... Blessed are the dead who die in the Lord. Then lo a white cloud, and seated on the cloud one like a son of man with a golden crown on his head.

Rev. 14:7, 9–10, 13–14

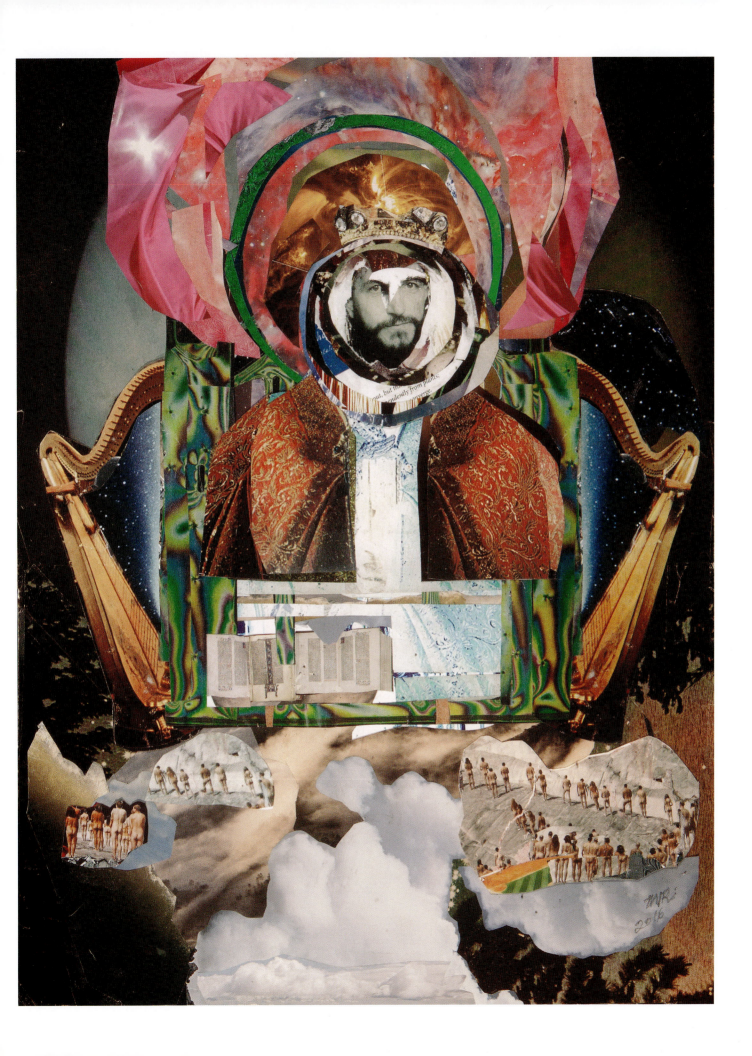

After this I looked and the temple of the tent of witness in heaven was opened and out of the temple came the seven angels with seven plagues, robed in pure bright linen ... And one of the four living creatures gave the seven angels seven golden bowls full of the wrath of God.

Rev. 15:5–7

The fourth angel poured his bowl on the sun, and it was allowed to scorch men with fire, and more were scorched by the fierce heat, and they cursed the name of God and they did not repent and give him glory.

Rev. 16:8–9

Then one of the seven angels said
I will show you the judgement
of the great harlot ... with whom
the kings of the earth committed
fornication ... The woman
was arrayed in purple and
scarlet, and bedecked with
gold and jewels and pearls,
holding in her hand a golden
cup full of abominations and
the impurities of her fornication.

Rev. 17:1–2,4

Then a mighty angel took us
a stone like a great millstone
and threw it into the sea, saying
'So shall Babylon the great city
be thrown down with violence.'

Rev. 18:21

After this I heard what seemed
to be the mighty voice of a great
multitude in heaven, crying
'Hallelujah!' Salvation and glory
and power belong to our God.
Let us rejoice and exult and give
him the glory, for the marriage
of the Lamb has come ...

Rev. 19:1, 6–7

Then I saw an angel coming down from heaven, holding in his hand the key of the bottomless pit and a great chain. And he seized the dragon, that ancient serpent, who is the Devil and Satan, and bound him for a thousand years and threw him into the pit, and shut it and sealed it over him, that he should deceive the nations no more.

Rev. 20:1–3

Then I saw a new heaven and a
new earth: for the first heaven
and first earth had passed
away, and the sea was no more.
And I saw the holy city, new
Jerusalem, come down out of
heaven from God, prepared as
a bride ... Behold the dwelling of
God is with men ... he will wipe
away every tear from their eyes.

Rev. 21:1–4

Do not seal up the words of the prophecy of this book, for the time is near. Let the evildoers still do evil, and the filthy still be filthy, and the righteous still do right, and the holy still be holy. Behold, I am coming soon bringing my recompense, to repay everyone for what he has done. I am the Alpha and Omega, the first and the last, the beginning and the end. 'I Jesus have sent my angel to you with this testimony for the churches. I am the root and offspring of David, the bright morning star' ... and let him who is thirsty come.

Rev. 22:10–13, 16–17